~

Let the Glory of the Lord come in!

~

Let the Glory of the Lord come in!

Love Covers A Multitude Of Sins

Lily Torres

Xulon Press

Xulon Press
2301 Lucien Way #415
Maitland, FL 32751
407.339.4217
www.xulonpress.com

© 2022 by Lily Torres

All rights reserved solely by the author. The author guarantees all contents are original and do not infringe upon the legal rights of any other person or work. No part of this book may be reproduced in any form without the permission of the author.

Due to the changing nature of the Internet, if there are any web addresses, links, or URLs included in this manuscript, these may have been altered and may no longer be accessible. The views and opinions shared in this book belong solely to the author and do not necessarily reflect those of the publisher. The publisher therefore disclaims responsibility for the views or opinions expressed within the work.

Unless otherwise indicated, Scripture quotations taken from the New King James Version (NKJV). Copyright © 1982 by Thomas Nelson, Inc. Used by permission. All rights reserved.

Paperback ISBN-13: 978-1-66285-704-1

Ebook ISBN-13: 978-1-66285-705-8

THIS BOOK IS DEDICATED TO MY BELOVED FATHER, JOSE ESTRELLA.

Table of Contents

Chapter 1: Rough Childhood 1

Chapter 2: Abusive Relationships 7

Chapter 3: God Always Provides 11

Chapter 4: Changing Lives. 18

Chapter 5: Love From God and a Husband. 22

Chapter 6: Leap of Faith. 28

Chapter 7: Answered Prayers and Forgiveness. 32

Chapter 1:
Rough Childhood

I remember when my father, Jose, spread open the kitchen curtains and would say, "Let the glory of the Lord come in." He would open the curtains whenever he would study the Bible.

My father grew up with street gangs from the age of eight. He met my mother, Aida, in New York and married her when he was thirty-five years old. A female Pentecostal pastor married them. I was their firstborn.

My mother would say to her friends and family that my father would have preferred if I had been a boy. I kept hearing this over and over during my childhood. I never felt that I was accepted as their child, especially after all my siblings were born. My parents would often keep me home from school so I could babysit whenever they ran their errands or whenever my father had his psychiatric appointments.

My father was strict with all of us, especially with me since I was developing into a young woman. He would tell my brother, "Miguel, if you see her talking with a boy, just slap her." I told Miguel, "If you slap me, I will beat you." Miguel never dared to slap me.

I was afraid of my father. We all were afraid of him. He strived to be a good family man when he was attending church. Pastor Lorenzo took a liking to my father, and the two grew close. My father preached on the streets whenever we had street services. My father would sing "Christ is the Lily of the Valley" in Spanish during service.

One day during a service, Lorenzo preached and said that men should be more disciplined in the things of the Lord. My father took offense to this as Lorenzo had noticed that my father was checking out a woman who passed by the church bus. My father said, "That's it, I am not going to come back to this church." We all knew what would happen next.

It was a matter of time before my father would go out and drink. My father went out to drink shortly after leaving the church. My mother would hide knives, even the butterknives, to keep us safe. This was a habit whenever he went out drinking.

My father would come home drunk and call out, "Aida! Bring some food!" My mother would scurry as quickly as she could to bring him food. Before he ate, he would have one of us taste the food. My mother had tried to poison him and his friends one time when she was forced to cook chicken soup for them. Ever since then, he did not trust her.

My father would threaten my mother with a machete at times. Many nights when my father came home, he would say, "I see demons in this house," and he would chase all of us out of the house with a baseball bat. We would end up staying overnight at the neighbors whenever that happened.

This continued for most weekends. He also would threaten neighbors and friends. When he got into trouble with the law, our family would start going to church. When that happened, I would feel a sense of relief. I finally was able to sleep through the night because he was sober.

Proverbs 28:13 *"He that covereth his sins shall not prosper: but whoso confesseth and forsaketh them shall have mercy."*

When my father was sober, we had great times. He would cook, do puzzles, and study the Bible. He would have books and the Bible spread out on the kitchen table every day. While he was in church, he did not drink but would still smoke and hide it from the church.

Home was a happy and stable place when my dad and mom went to church, and we had fun experiences. We went to an amusement park called Great Adventure. We also went fishing using soda cans with the fishing lines tied around the soda cans and would catch and fill a five-gallon bucket full of fish.

When my father was in church, he developed a close relationship with the pastor and then, in turn, was permitted to preach and sing. My father would preach great messages. He was very intelligent, given that he only had a fourth-grade education. I loved when he sang "Cristo El Lirio de los Lirios." He had such passion when he sang.

Our home was peaceful but strict. I was not allowed to have friends over or go to any events with children my age. I went to church and learned what not to do and to be fearful of God. It was like I had better obey God. If not, something bad would happen to me.

My mother would pray a lot when my father would go out binge drinking and never stopped attending church. She would get my brothers and sister ready for church and walked in the middle of winter while pushing a stroller holding my sister, Miriam, with my brother, Miguel, and I walking alongside.

There was such fear in the house that you could touch it. We would hide anything that my father could use to threaten my mother. He would come home so drunk that he would start seeing things. He would start threatening to hurt my mother and then chase all of us out of the house. There were times that he would slam the machete against the kitchen table to show his dominance. I did not sleep in fear of never waking up.

My father would show up drunk at the church. The pastor would start publicly praying and rebuking demonic forces. My father yelled at the pastor, saying, "You are the one who has the demon!" He forced my mother, my siblings, and I to get in the car with him drunk. I witnessed my father slamming my mother's head against the wall, saying, "I know you have a lover in that church!"

I made a promise to myself that I would never let a man lay his hands on me like that. I also closed my heart out to everyone. Something inside of me died, and I wanted it to remain dead. I did not want to feel anymore.

Isaiah 28:18 *"Your covenant with death will be annulled; your agreement with realm of the dead will not stand. When the overwhelming scourge sweeps by, you will be beaten down by it."*

As Miguel and I became teenagers, things worsened at home. My father turned his anger to Miguel. He would say, "You are not a man until I say you are a man!" He would often whip him with a belt and coaxial cable. I know how that hurt because I had to endure it as well.

Miguel ran away from the house when he turned seventeen and went to live with our Aunt Lola. Miguel only came back to get his belongings. My father said to him, "I am going to put you in a foster home." Aunt Lola responded, "Not if he has family." Miguel gathered his belongings, got in Lola's car, and left.

I attended a vocational high school. I was focused on getting my education so I could become a secretary. My mother wanted me to become a nurse. She would say, "I want you to be like your cousins." She admired my cousins and wished I looked like them. My cousins were light-skinned, beautiful, and confident.

I was not on a mission to become like them. My focus was to finish school, get an education, and get out of the house. My mother was stressed handling seven children, even with me helping her. I was expected to take care of my brothers and sister and keep up with the house.

My mother was closer to my brothers and sister and treated them like her children. I wanted that kind of relationship with her, but I never expected it because I felt I was never good enough for her.

I developed asthma and had a hard time breathing. My father felt compassion for me. He researched and came up with an elixir. He gave my mother a recipe of aloe, onion, honey, and cod liver oil. My mother would give me two tablespoons of this elixir twice a day. That taste would last in my mouth for the entire day, but it did work, and I had fewer asthma attacks until they stopped altogether.

My father showed me that he loved me but had this demon that would come out every time he got drunk.

I met and started dating my first boyfriend, Juan, during my high school senior year. He met my father. My father was not too happy about this. He would watch when I came home from seeing him and would strike me with his arm. That did not stop me. My parents hit me daily, and I got used to it.

I continued to see Juan. I entered a stage where I did not care anymore about my father's threats and what he did. He said that he would put me six feet under, but that did not stop me.

During the summer, my parents sent me to my grandmother's home so I could forget about my boyfriend. My mother was in tears when I left. I was shocked and numbed to see her like that. My dad wanted me to kiss him on the cheek when they said goodbye. I reluctantly did.

During my stay with my grandparents, I enjoyed my grandfather because he was a jokester. One day, he said he had a present for me and gave me his chewed-up tobacco. I didn't mind the joke; he was just trying to be funny.

My grandmother was distant from me. She never conversed with me, and I barely interacted with my grandfather. My grandmother wanted me to go back to my parents' home. I then was sent to live with my Uncle Pablo for a few weeks. I found out that my grandmother was talking about me, saying I had the music hidden in me, meaning that I was hiding something. She was very suspicious of me.

Finally, graduation came. I was so excited! My boyfriend's mother got me a pink dress to wear, and I felt important. I received two medals for high honors, considering that I had to learn how to read and write in Spanish at the age of fifteen after moving to Puerto Rico from New York because my dad and mom wanted to have a homestead in Puerto Rico.

At my graduation, my boyfriend's mom was the only one there to support me along with my boyfriend. I then came home and was able to change into the prom dress that my cousin had given to me. My dad saw my outfit and my haircut. "Look at her," he said. "She looks like a prostitute, and her hair is cut."

After graduation, I was still dating my boyfriend, and had a job selling timeshares. My dad expected me to give him half of my paycheck to help the family out. I never did give any money, and two months later, I moved out.

Chapter 2:
Abusive Relationships

Proverbs 14:12 *"There is a way that appears to be right, but in the end, it leads to death."*

After moving out, I was happy as I escaped the horrors of living in that environment. I did not attend church since I had no friends or any ties to the church. I had run away with Juan, but I did not know whether I loved him or not. Honestly, I did not know what love was. I saw him as an escape and told myself that anything would be better than living at home.

My relationship with Juan did not last long. He did not love me, either. It was four long years of him selling drugs and trying to get me to use drugs. Thank God, I never was attracted to that.

I lived a life with no meaning or purpose. I was empty and didn't even know it. I often fantasized about having loving parents who would one day come and rescue me. I mastered how to disguise the pain, as I had learned when I was growing up.

I kept going in and out of abusive relationships and was attracted to the worst type of men. I remember that sometime ago, I had said that I would never let anyone hurt me like my father hurt my mother, but there I was in that same boat. I could not figure out why I was attracted to these bad boys.

I was visiting a small church in the city and met Pastor Michelle. I visited her, and we talked about my life. She said, "I want you to write down any hurt that your father caused you and write the words, 'I forgive you,' next to it, and send this to your father."

I immediately started writing, for there was a lot to say, and I ended up writing two pages' worth of material. I handed the letter to my mother in a sealed envelope to give to my father. He and I had grown apart, and we did not talk. I didn't think I hated him, but neither he nor I could be bothered. My mother said, "Your father thought that this was strange what you did."

I moved to another town to escape another abusive relationship. This man would drink just like my father and would repeatedly recant his sad stories. I was not compassionate at all and would get up and tell him that I was tired of hearing his sad stories.

This got him angry with me, and he dragged me to the bathroom and held a pair of scissors to my throat. I thought it was the last day of my life. I managed to escape and ran down the hallway and got in my car.

As I was driving uphill, he was hanging onto the hood of my car. I stopped the car and saw a neighbor looking at us. I rolled the window down just enough to ask the neighbor to call the police. At that point, he left and went back to his apartment. When the police officer arrived, he asked what had happened, wrote down something on his tablet, and told me that I could go to a shelter if I wanted to leave.

I gathered my things and went to a domestic violence unit. I noticed that the ladies there treated the place like a vacation resort. My mother told me the man I was running from was contacting her, trying to find out where I was. I did not feel safe staying in that local shelter, so I moved to another shelter in a different town just to get away from this crazy man.

At the new shelter, the women there had their own issues. The workers were nice and made me feel comfortable and accepted. It was a nice break that I had needed for a long time.

I was able to find an apartment in housing and had a friend in the neighborhood who I had met at the shelter. I was going to college and was happy. I had a new life, nice apartment, and felt I was doing something productive.

My only support was my friend, Jackie. I was far from my family and did not receive much support. I would talk to my mother on the phone. She was nice, but for some reason, I was not able to connect with her emotionally.

Jackie started dating someone, and we barely hung out as a result, so I was feeling a little lonely. She then moved out of the neighborhood soon after. I was so alone with no one to talk to.

I went ahead and signed up for a dating event over the radio and that is how I met John. I did not fall in love with him, although I enjoyed his company and was attracted to his stability. We dated for a couple of weeks when I discovered that I was pregnant. I was devastated being that I was a single mother.

We both had unresolved issues from our pasts and had so many fights, but we tried to make it work. We would break up and get back together, and I would receive constant calls from him asking me to go back to him. he would then threaten to have our son taken away if I did not go back to him.

I was devastated and almost had a nervous breakdown. My neighbor, Towanda, stopped by, which was out of blue. She saw my condition and offered to stay with my children so I could go out and get some air.

Everything hit me at once. I could not stop crying and felt like dying. Towanda would often check on me. She then asked if her mother could call me. I agreed. I got a call from her mother, who asked if I wanted to accept Jesus as my Lord and Savior, and I agreed.

I attended a vibrant church. The church leaders would say that the service was over when the Holy Ghost said it was over. I enjoyed the Friday night services. The Friday night service would start at 7:00 p.m. and last until 11:00 p.m. at times. I had people praying over me and anointing oil on my forehead. I loved the scent of it. There was so much weight lifted off from me that I felt I was in the clouds after service.

There were many times when I felt so much was wrong with me that I did not know where to begin. I thought I was so far gone that not even God could fix me.

I saw these Christians singing and praising God, but I felt like an outsider looking in. I was could not understand what they felt as they were at a much deeper level than me. I felt I could never reach that level and felt the same way when I lived at home. I was not good enough and would never amount to anything, as my parents often would tell me.

My mother wanted me to be pretty like my cousins and act like them. At the time, I didn't think too much of it. My father told me that I would end up with five children and an abusive husband. I would repeatedly hear that in my head. I did not like myself and would hide my identity. I had non-Christian friends and could be my dysfunctional self around them. That was my comfort zone.

Chapter 3:
God Always Provides

Proverbs 27:7 *"The full soul loatheth an honeycomb; but to the hungry soul every bitter thing is sweet"*

I was a lonely single mom. I felt I was doing something good by going to church, believing that would improve my life, but my loneliness overwhelmed me. I did not know how to make friends at church. I loved the environment, but I could not connect with anyone as a peer. I felt that Pastor Michelle did not like me for some reason.

I began staying home from church. Two precious ladies were nice to me that I met at that church, Sister Petra and Sister Nellie. Sister Nellie would call me and say, "I missed you at church. Here is what we went over." She would pray for me and called me every week for six months. I would visit Sister Nellie, who was always excited to see me.

Isaiah 43:2 *"When thou passest through the water, I will be with thee; and through the rivers, they shall not overflow thee: when thou walkest through the fire, thou shall not be burned; neither shall the flame kindle upon thee."*

It had been a couple of months since I had stopped going and was attending a different church. After a year, I stopped going altogether. I still had respect for God but could not trust Him as I did not trust my father.

I went back to John. I lived with him for a while after having my second child with him. We had an on-and-off relationship. Things worsened between us. He would often kick me out of his house and say, "Please don't leave," under the same breath. I did not get any compliments or feel loved by him. On the other hand, I did not love him either.

I finally decided I had enough. I left his home and moved to an apartment with my children. He then filed for custody. I had no money, so I had no attorney to fight him back.

Toward the end of the custody battle, I finally qualified to get a free attorney and was scheduled for a psychological evaluation. The evaluator seemed as if he had his mind already made up as he asked me questions about my past.

It was on Monday afternoon at 3:00 p.m. when I got the call from my attorney, saying, "The psychologist recommended for John to have custody of the boys." I was shocked. I felt that time stopped, and I felt as if I was out of my body as I left my workplace. I did not tell a soul. I felt so embarrassed. I felt that the court system ripped my children from my womb. I could not stop crying.

I was devastated. I did not want to get out of bed. I would stay up until 3:00 a.m. and only slept three hours a day.

I went to court that day. I was there but felt I was living a nightmare. During the seven-hour trial, my mother was not allowed in the hearing. The only evidence against me was that I had moved several times and had several relationships. John had his own home and had lived there for years. So, the judge said he was giving custody to the father, and he called me mean-spirited because I fought him in court.

When I left that courtroom, I felt like a train had run over me. The attorney who represented me asked if I could join him for coffee. He wanted to make sure that I was okay and assured me I would rebound from this. I felt that the Lord used him to tell me this, even though I felt my life would be a major mess.

God Always Provides

I worked for an agency in the social work field and loved my job. I had always wanted to be a social worker. I enjoyed helping disadvantaged people. My supervisor, Mary, was nice. I felt comfortable with Mary as she was intelligent, caring, and comforting. I confided in her and told her what had happened. She was outraged that my boys were taken from me for no real reason.

I was not sleeping and did not want to face the world. I wanted to stay home and wallow in my pain and shame. Mary would call me and insist that I come into work. She said, "I don't care what time you show up. Please just come in."

I would spend hours talking to Mary about my feelings, and she would patiently listen. She was a kind soul to me at the time.

My first day back to work was difficult. I did not know how to face life. Beth, my co-worker, was a bitter woman and did not like me. She was not well-liked at the office. When I came to the office the day after the court hearing, she gave me a big hug and said, "I am so sorry this happened to you." I was taken back by this. She was nice to me from that day forward.

At that point, everyone knew what had happened. My shameful secret was out, yet no one had judged me. Instead, I received support and sympathy from everyone. Someone even asked me if it was true that they had taken my kids from me for no real reason.

When I went back to work, the first call I received was from a ninety-year-old foster grandmother named Nikki. She had a son who killed his wife and children before killing himself, yet she remained a happy lady.

She said, "When I get up in the morning, I thank my Daddy God for everything He has done for me and drink my black coffee." I said to myself, "She went through something worse than me." Hearing her voice gave me hope and looking at her example gave me the courage to go on.

I felt that going to work was like being with family. They were such a great support. I was smiled at, I felt valued and accepted. I was so depleted of love and acceptance. One day, Mary said something very significant to me. She said, "You are a wonderful woman." I almost cried; no one had ever said such a nice thing about me. I thought I was the worst human being on the face of the earth.

One evening after work when I came home and opened my mail, I saw a letter from "Domestic Relations," and the appointment date was set.

John took me to court for child support, and we had a conference meeting with the support representative. I was ordered to pay $375 a month. I thought that was a lot considering I was only making eleven dollars an hour and had to take care of my daughter. Her father was nowhere to be found.

John said that the amount was too little. He had his attorney take me before the judge to demand more money. We appeared before the judge, then it was imposed for me to pay $450 month. This left me with only $758 a month for my daughter and me to live on. I cried in the courtroom, and John's attorney mocked me in front of everyone.

It was hard for me to continue working in the office. Since the agency was in the courthouse, I would bump into the custody conference officer. He would mock me and give me weird looks. I thought about reporting him, but I chose not to.

It was Christmas time. By that time, I had gotten used to going to the Salvation Army to get free food to supplement my groceries. I wanted my children to have a good Christmas; however, I still felt ashamed and hoped that none of my co-workers would see me standing in line.

I qualified for the food pantry but was not sure if I qualified for the Christmas Angel Tree. Most government help would go by income regardless of child support payments. I asked the Salvation Army if I qualified for the Christmas Angel Tree. They gave me an application, and I signed up.

I was embarrassed as I stood in line because the local news camera was there. I made sure that I hid from them. I did not want anyone recognizing me. I then went to pick up my number, and the woman who attended me said that a family has decided to adopt me. I did not know what that meant.

When it came time for me to pick the gifts, I was overwhelmed to find so many gifts. My daughter got bike and clothes, and my boys got clothes too. I even got clothes my size and a gift card for a beauty salon. I wondered who had done this. I had so many gifts that it took three trips in my vehicle to get all of them home. I was happy and overwhelmed by it all. We had a great Christmas.

At the office, the executive director, administrator, and every head of each department got together and gave me a gift card for Walmart and a gift card to the mall. I also received a big box with a turkey, potatoes, pumpkin pie, and other food.

I never had anyone, much less a group, be so giving to me. I was happy knowing that people did care, and God cared too.

I tried to keep my financial struggles a secret. I felt so ashamed of myself, but it was no longer a secret. Everybody knew.

I had a dream one night that I was crossing over to the parking lot. I saw some black horses that wanted to charge at me, but something held them back. The more I looked at them, the more ferocious they became. I felt like God was telling me that the more I looked at my problems, the bigger they would become.

Psalm 91:11 *"For he shall give his angels charge over thee, to keep thee in all thy ways."*

I was invited by one of the volunteers from work, Sonia, who was also my mother's friend, to go with her to her church. I gladly accepted her invitation. As I continued to attend, I started liking the church. This helped me to grow in my faith.

I loved the church environment but did not have the love of Jesus in my heart. My heart was like hard stone and did not even realize it. For so many years, I would smile and be nice to people, but I never let anyone know the real me, not even Mary.

God was patient with me, though. Many times, I failed Him, but He continued to show His love toward me. I had a hard time trusting Him as I was confused about my upbringing.

Ezekiel 36:26 *"A new heart also will I give you, and a new spirit will I put within you: and I will take away the stony heart out of your flesh, and I will give you an heart of flesh."*

Sonia and I became friends. She would call me and invite me over to her apartment. She gave me Christian music. I would listen to it in my car and at home, enjoying the wonderful worship music. Suddenly, I raised my arms and worshiped God all by myself. I never felt a love so great like it before. Tears streamed down my face. It was so powerful!

I would watch Christian ministries on TV. I reached out to a ministry for prayer, and they quickly responded. I also got free materials from them. The materials I received were healing for me and helped me get closer to God.

From that point forward, I was able to worship God, and two weeks later, I received the Holy Spirit. It was like a veil fell off my eyes. I was able to better understand the Bible. My prayers were more specific, and I felt God's presence. I believe that when a group or someone is praying for you, God gets involved. I felt there was a breakthrough in removing the barrier to getting closer to God.

I still dealt with low self-esteem and shame. I was embarrassed and ashamed of how I became a single mom, paying child support, and with children from different fathers. I was broke, lonely, and felt worthless. I did not feel that I fit in the church. I saw women, and they had their lives together. I felt I could never measure up to them. If people knew the real me, they would judge me.

Chapter 4:
Changing Lives

Matthew 6:33 *"But seek ye first the kingdom of God, and his righteousness; and all these things shall be added unto you."*

I started working a second part-time job because I was living in an apartment that became unaffordable for me when I started paying child support. My friend Abigail was moving and recommended I take her apartment, which was one hundred dollars less a month and nicer. Abigail gave me curtains, pots and pans, and a green swivel La-Z-Boy chair.

My mother knew a couple who was running a halfway house. The couple would give my mother free chicken for me and the children, I was getting free clothes from churches, and I always had money to pay my bills and rent. My car, which had a lot of miles on it, ran excellent. I felt that God was taking care of me, but I was still bitter about everything that had happened to me.

After having financial trouble, not being able to keep money in my bank, and getting many overdraft fees, I quickly learned how to balance my budget. I felt that God told me to give Him what I had left as take-home. How I understood it, I was to trust Him with what I had to provide for my daughter and me and my boys when they came over. I was able to keep a tight budget by being creative in my cooking, looking for sales, and combining my meals with food pantry items. It was not healthy, but we were fed, and the bills were paid.

When I started paying $450 for child support, I was left with $758 a month to live on. This was tight, considering my other bills included:

- Electricity = $25
- Rent = $400
- Cable = $30
- Insurance $75
- Groceries = $100
- Church Offering = about $40

I was left with eighty-eight dollars for gas for my car but tried to save some of that money in my bank account. Thankfully, my job was only three miles from my apartment, so my gas expense was not much.

I felt that God wanted me to forgive John from snatching my children from me. I prayed to God to help me forgive him. I needed Him to help because it was difficult. As I prayed, I felt this evil presence in my room breathing deeply. I kept praying until it went away. Looking back, I think it was a demon called unforgiveness.

Forgiveness did not come quickly, but I was on that path. I would cry every time I had to go back home after visiting my children. I was not included in their school conferences and other school-related activities.

It was difficult for me to see my children because I had no money to entertain them when they came over. We would go to church on Sunday mornings. I would take them to parks during the summertime, and during the wintertime, we would go to the library to use the computer since I did not have one at home.

Philippians 4:8 *" Finally, brethren, whatsoever things are true, whatsoever things are honest, whatsoever things are just, whatsoever things are lovely, whatsoever things are of good report; if there be any virtue, and if there be any praise, think on these things."*

It would infuriate me when I heard that my sons would go to expensive amusement parks, and I was only able to pack peanut butter sandwiches and take them to local parks. I would think, *Yeah, sure. Must be nice for John not working and having me give him money every month so he can have a life of luxury.* I felt he was taking food from my daughter's mouth.

I felt anxious and worthless most of the time. I remembered that dream I had with the horses. The dream kept coming to my thoughts. After a while, I made up my mind not to think about negative thoughts. It was a hard habit to break. I started spending time praying and growing closer to God and not on negative things.

One afternoon when I went to work, Mary called me into her office. She asked me to close the door then told me that she and the executive director at the office were promoting me so I could get a raise. I was so surprised and overwhelmed that they had gone out of their way to financially help me. Mary felt bad that I had to work a second part-time job to make ends meet.

My part-time job involved me taking care of this elderly woman who was bitter toward life. She liked my presence but was kind of rough with me. While cooking and cleaning for her, I came across this cute calendar with a cat lying on its back that said, "If you are flat on your back, look up." That profoundly spoke to me. God would talk to me even through a calendar. It was amazing!

After a couple of months, I was able to quit my second job. The elderly woman I was working for was placed in a nursing home, and on my last day with her, she gave me a Bible cover and a beautiful necklace. I was surprised to receive these gifts. I truly was not expecting them.

When I did announce that I was quitting, the elderly woman's daughter gave me an extra week of pay and included a thank-you note for me, thanking me for taking good care of her mother. I kept that card because it meant the world to me.

I often thought my life was insignificant and messed up. I never thought my interaction with people would matter. I loved serving people but never thought about how my interaction would impact them. I came to find out that even though this elderly woman did not express at the time how grateful she was for having me, I was a blessing to her all along.

That was a pivotal moment for me. I never knew I could impact someone like that. It made me feel so good knowing that I am valuable.

Chapter 5:
Love from God and a Husband

Romans 8:28 *"And we know that in all things God works for the good of those who love Him, who have been called according to His purpose."*

I started regularly attending a different church. The church was open every day of the week for prayer. This took my walk with God to a whole new level.

I was interested in serving the church. The pastor required me to read Christian books, complete homework assignments, and turn those in. He wanted to know how committed I was. It was a struggle for me. I did not like reading, but for me to serve, I had to do it, and it had to be completed in a timely fashion.

I finally got it done and got involved in teaching Bible studies and greeting. After a while, I asked the pastor if I could facilitate a single mothers support group.

I wanted to help single moms. I felt that people looked down upon women when they were single moms. The world would say, "Doesn't she believe in birth control?" or "She should have kept her legs closed." I felt condemned, and my family looked down on me as well.

I felt fulfilled in serving the church. It was exciting for me to help other women out, especially those who lost their children and felt worthless. I met a woman whose boyfriend got custody of her children.

She reminded me of me when I was young in the Lord. She would keep her eyes down and looked for people's approval.

I could imagine what the woman at the well (John 4:4–26) felt. She probably felt ashamed of herself, being married five times, and the man she was with was not her husband. When Jesus met her, He never shamed her but did point out her sin.

I was with this church for almost three years and had made no friends. I had a woman that wanted to befriend me, and I said to myself, "Finally." She watched my daughter while I was at work. I would spend time with her at her home.

I truly thought she was my friend. I discovered a notebook in my daughter's room and decided to read it. I was devastated to find out what she was writing. I shared it with the pastor and my friend.

A couple of weeks later, all the leaders at the church found out. One of the women said to me, "I see you praying with such power for people, but you ignore your daughter." I immediately confronted her by saying, "That is not true."

Slowly after that, the women treated me like I was less than a reputable Christian woman. They would get together for fellowship, and I was not invited. They would say that my daughter must join a class, as if they were trying to force me to comply. The youth leader asked me in a condescending way, "Where is her father?" I felt terrible, ashamed, and beat down all at once. I thought about leaving the church, but I had ministries I was involved in.

One night, I was sleeping with the TV on and momentarily woke up. I heard a minister praying and saying, "I see a woman with dark hair thinking about leaving a church. The Lord is telling you to leave that church." When I heard this, my jaw dropped. Wow, God was directly talking to me!

I called the pastor to tell him that the women were talking about me. The pastor said maybe they were just sharing information amongst themselves. I told him since this was not being addressed, I was leaving the church.

I heard a Christian song that resonated in my spirit; this song was about freedom. I felt this overwhelming peace and joy as I was singing as if I was liberated from the enemy's claw with his condemnation.

I then started visiting other churches and did not depart from the Lord. I realized that leaving a church does not mean leaving God; what it meant was putting God above the churches. I believed in godly community, but if I did not feel connected, maybe it was not the right community for me.

I heard churches say, "Let a man find you." I read Proverbs 18:22, *"He who finds a wife finds what is good and receives favor from the Lord."* I heard churches take this out of context, stating that women had no business pursuing a relationship.

Thank God that I would go against the grain at times and take what people said with a grain of salt. I tried the singles group for a while, but these so-called "Christian" men looked down on me since I had children from different men and had been in several relationships. I felt, though, that there was one out there for me who would love me.

I had a minister who asked me some time ago, "Have you asked God for a husband?" I told him I had. He followed up with, "But did you ask what specifically you are looking for?"

That had me thinking. I wrote down in a journal a prayer request asking God what kind of husband I would like to have. I requested one who loved Him, loved my children, and one who would be kind and considerate.

When I was ministering in the single mothers' support group, I took a cardboard pencil box and made a slit on top of it so that women could slide in prayer requests for the Lord. I felt at that time that the Lord asked me, *"What about you? Ask me for a husband."* I debated with God and told Him I shouldn't, but I felt that God insisted that I do this. I wrote on a three-by-five index card my request: I would like a husband.

Years went by. I talked to my friend, Elizabeth, and asked, "Do you think it would be a sin if I sign up with a dating site?" She said, "I do not see anything wrong with that." I respected her opinion since she was a God-fearing woman. I went ahead and signed up online. Within a month, a man named Anthony expressed interest. We communicated and called each other every day. I said to God that if he proposed, I would marry him. I wasn't sure where that had come from because I was not thinking about that before I prayed. I bombarded this man with many questions and tested him to know his intentions.

About a month after we started talking, I told him that I had several relationships, had children from different fathers, and had lost custody of two of my children. I felt I might as well be rejected now than later. His response was, "That does not matter. What matters is who you are now." That brought tears to my eyes. He did not see it because we were on the phone, but his words were so healing for me.

After dating Anthony for six weeks, he proposed to me on a walking trail on a beautiful spring morning. He knelt on one knee and asked, "Will you marry me?" I never had anyone treat me with such dignity before.

We were engaged on April 26, 2010 and set our wedding date for August 16, 2010. I was so overjoyed! I even got a bridal shower from my co-workers! The only problem we were facing is that I lived in Reading and he lived in Pittsburgh. One of us would have to move in order to live in one household. We decided to move forward with our relationship being that we felt comfortable with each other and enjoyed each other. I figured that we would do a long-distance marriage for a while, and we were ok with that.

When I got that engagement ring, I could not stop looking at it. It was not the engagement ring; it was the man who placed that ring on my finger. I was glowing and happy.

One of my co-workers asked, "Who is the lucky man?" That melted my heart. I had never heard anyone say that to me. I always thought I was never good enough. It is interesting how God would validate me through people or other means. I will never forget what she said to me.

God's love has always surrounded me. I just had to recognize, appreciate, and be thankful about it.

The wedding day was fast approaching. I felt that the Lord spoke to me as I was trying on my wedding dress. He told me to get the pencil box with the prayer request that I had written when I was facilitating the single mothers support group.

I had forgotten about the box. I found it and pulled out my prayer request. To my amazement, the request was written on the same day at the same time years ago as the same time and day I was trying on my dress.

I was so amazed at how detailed God was, and everything fit in His plan if I let Him direct my life! God was telling me, *"You see? I have answered your prayer."* God never stops amazing me!

Our day finally came. It was on a Monday. I tried getting churches to marry us but could not find one. I went ahead and scheduled our ceremony with the district justice. Monday was the only day available.

Most of the attendees were my co-workers and some family members. My photographer was my twelve-year-old son. He did an excellent job recording the wedding on his cell phone. The ring bearer was my husband's oldest son. There was so much love, and it was so special!

Our reception was at my mother's home. I cooked lasagna. My new husband and I were financially struggling, yet the table looked so beautiful with the Dollar Tree décor. My friend, who was not a regular church attendee, gifted me a Dominican cake. A co-worker gifted cash, and my other co-workers gave us a gas card for over one hundred dollars. The wedding was at a budget, like a teeny tiny budget, but it was so rich in love. People said that I was glowing.

The wedding was over, and we went on our honeymoon. I felt so happy like I was walking on clouds. When our honeymoon was over, we then had to face the reality that we could not live together in the same household. He lived in Pittsburgh, and I lived in Reading. We decided to marry each other anyway because we felt that we fit together. I got a journal at Ollie's. My husband and I started writing in it our petitions to God. One of our petitions was that we would be under one roof.

Chapter 6:
Leap of Faith

Habakkuk 2:2 *"And the Lord answered me, and said, Write the vision, and make it plain upon tables, that he may run that readeth it."*

After we married, we continued seeing each other. We were five hours apart, but I felt close to my husband, and we trusted each other.

The Lord was dealing with me. I felt He was telling me to move in with my husband. I asked Him, "How can this happen when I am paying child support, have a great-paying job, a house, and my children?" I was fine with the long-distance relationship after waiting for God to answer my prayer.

At work, I felt this excruciating pain in my lower back as I was lifting boxes to deliver to the food pantry. I thought I had twisted my back, and eventually, the pain would go away; however, it got worse overtime.

I went to see a doctor. The x-rays were ordered, and I found out that I had injured my lower back by carrying those heavy boxes. I asked the doctor if he could give me a note for work so that I would not have to lift any more heavy boxes.

We had a new administration at work, so my old supervisors were gone. When I went to present my doctor's note to human resources, they denied it and told me that the only way I could continue with my job was if I continued lifting heavy boxes and deliver food pantries to clients. I felt trapped. I was put on short-term disability. I did not know what to do as I could not go back to work. I told my husband that I am moving to Pittsburgh, and he was astonished. He asked, "What about the house? What about your job? What about your children?" I said, "I don't know, but I felt led to move to Pittsburgh." I planned to continue seeing my children and rent my home.

After five months of disability, the doctor refused to continue signing the disability notes. It was time for me to go back to work under those conditions.

I thank God that He always provides and is a God who always steps in right on time. I applied for a job in Pittsburgh. It paid a lot less than I was making, but I decided to go for it at the time. I wasn't too happy about the type of job. I applied for it, and then after thinking about it, I withdrew my application.

I continued applying for different jobs and could not find one that was suitable. After a couple of months, I asked the recruiter if the same job was available, and she said yes. God was so amazing! My husband and I were both astonished at how this happened. Normally when someone turns down a job offer, no other chance is given.

I started working at my new job, and my daughter then started her new school. She made friends, and we were happy. I was able to rent my house, and everything was working fine, I was able to see my children monthly, and we made the best of it.

I was talking to the Lord and said, "Lord, this is so expensive just traveling like this and seeing my children. I don't know what to do, how to entertain them, and how should I feed them."

One day, I was driving down the interstate. I looked to the left and saw a big sign that said, "Camping." I mean I could have read that in my mind in slow motion. I said to myself, "Yes, I could do camping. I have never done camping in my life."

God was so great! He was teaching me a new skill! He was allowing certain things to take place in my life so I could step out of the boat. I went ahead and purchased a used tent from one of my co-workers at my new job and practiced setting it up. I got air mattresses, and we started camping.

We went to different camping sites. The tent sites were about twenty-five dollars a night. I set up the tent and blew up the air mattresses for all of us. My husband was reluctant, but he went along with it. My first-time camping was not a great experience. It was thundering. I said to everyone, "Quick, take the tent down!" as the winds blew. Next, came the heavy downpour. We had to wait until the storm passed to set up the tent again.

After learning how to camp with a tent, we began enjoying the experience. I brought food from home and cooked it on the grill. We went swimming, Anthony played basketball with my boys, and we played ping pong. I praised the Lord that during the summertime, spring, and fall, we were able to go camping.

During the wintertime, we just made the best of it. I brought my children to Pittsburgh on weekends. At times, I would just visit them during the day or stay at overnight hotels near where they were living. I praised God that He always provided and never failed me.

I had a 2000 Ford Taurus that had over 160,000 miles on it. I was driving about five hours one way once a month. I had this big faith in the Lord, and I dared not look to the left or right because it would cause me anxiety.

Years ago, when I first got saved, I used to worry about every little thing. I was afraid to look at my mail and look at my bank account given the circumstances I was living. The Lord kept giving me this Scripture: *"Take therefore no thought for the morrow: for the morrow shall take thought for the things of itself. Sufficient unto the day is the evil thereof.'* (Matthew 6:34).

People say that you see God as you see your parents. I did not have any faith in my parents. In my early young adult years, I was never close to anyone as no one was ever close to me when I was growing up. I lived at home, did as I was told, and stayed out of trouble just so I wouldn't get beaten.

That was the same way I was with God. I respected Him and tried to stay out of trouble just so I wouldn't get punished. I did not know what love was until I allowed God in my heart.

I had nowhere to turn to but to trust God, and this was one of the occasions. The Lord blessed me so much that the vehicle hardly had any mechanical problems.

I loaded that Ford Taurus so much with my camping equipment, food, and drinks that it scraped at the bottom every time I hit a bump. It was just like my mini travel trailer.

Chapter 7:
Answered Prayers and Forgiveness

Ecclesiastes 3:1 *"To every thing there is a season, and a time to every purpose under the heaven"*

I got a call from my mother that my father was in the hospital. I was able to contact him and went to visit him. He had suffered a heart attack. He was the type of man who never showed any weakness or illness.

When I went to visit him, he was frying chicken and making rice. He cooked well, better than my mother. I went to see him a couple of times. On one of my visits, he talked about his girlfriend. They had been together for twenty years, even while he was married to my mother. My parents were divorced for over a decade and he was living with his girlfriend.

I was burning on the inside, and he felt my discontent. That was the last visit in years. I tried to get a hold of him, but he was not interested in a relationship with me.

Years later, I got custody of one of my sons. It was a big adjustment for him. I was so scared that he might run away since he did not

want to leave his dad behind, given his dad's health condition. He then adjusted and was content living with us.

Six months later, I got custody of my other son. I thank God for answering my prayers and allowing me to be their full-time mom. I volunteered to take them to see their father monthly. I would stay at hotels or campgrounds while they visited their father.

One day, I got a call from my mother telling me that my father was given a little time to live. She gave me his phone number. I called him; he said that he was fine and there was no need for me to come over. I heard his girlfriend say in the background, "Please come and see him."

My husband and one of my sons went with me to see him. When we went to his apartment, he was walking from the kitchen with a cup of coffee. The first thing he said to me was, "Please forgive me for everything I did to you." He said this five times as if one time was not enough. I told him, repeatedly, of course, I forgave him. I prayed for his salvation for nearly two years. I asked God to not let him depart from this earth until he made peace with God. I told him, "I have forgiven you a long time ago."

He offered me a cup of coffee. I said no. I wanted him to sit down before he fell. He had a hard time walking; he was losing his balance. He did not like to show any weakness. During our hour and a half visit, he allowed my husband and I to pray over him to reconcile with God. It was so powerful. I thank God for that opportunity.

That hour and a half visit was great. We laughed, and it felt good interacting with him in a healthy way. I never thought that I would have that opportunity.

When I went back home, I cried tears of joy for what the Lord had done. One of my family members told me that my father said, "I really ruined your lives." That right there was what he needed to realize. He needed God's forgiveness. If I did not forgive him, God was not able to use me to lead him back to Christ.

My father was dying. I prayed that God would take away the fear of death so he could peacefully pass away. Anthony and my family went to see him after he passed. He looked so peaceful, like nothing had ever happened to him.

John 11:26 *"And whosoever liveth and believeth in me shall never die. Believest thou this?"*

God allowed me to see my father in a vision: He was flying up to heaven in a beautiful white gown enlaced with silver and gold. He looked young and healthy.

1 Peter 4:8 *"And above all things have fervent charity among yourselves: for charity shall cover the multitude of sins."*

I know what it really means to the let the glory of the Lord come in. Let God come in!